ADDRESS BOOK
# NAUTICAL

The Pocket Size Address Book

www.journalsrus.com

Address Book Nautical
© 2016 Ciparum LLC
All rights reserved.
ISBN-10:1-63589-061-6
ISBN-13:978-1-63589-061-7

# Table of Content

| Name | Page | | Name | Page |
|------|------|------|------|------|
| | | | | |
| | | | | |
| | | | | |
| | | | | |
| | | | | |
| | | | | |
| | | | | |
| | | | | |
| | | | | |
| | | | | |
| | | | | |
| | | | | |
| | | | | |
| | | | | |
| | | | | |
| | | | | |
| | | | | |
| | | | | |
| | | | | |
| | | | | |
| | | | | |
| | | | | |
| | | | | |
| | | | | |

| Name | Page | | Name | Page |
|------|------|--|------|------|
|  |  |  |  |  |
|  |  |  |  |  |
|  |  |  |  |  |
|  |  |  |  |  |
|  |  |  |  |  |
|  |  |  |  |  |
|  |  |  |  |  |
|  |  |  |  |  |
|  |  |  |  |  |
|  |  |  |  |  |
|  |  |  |  |  |
|  |  |  |  |  |
|  |  |  |  |  |
|  |  |  |  |  |

THIS PAGE WAS
INTENTIONALLY
LEFT BLANK

**NAME**............................................................................

ADDRESS.......................................................................

.....................................................................................

MOBILE # (Cell).............................................................

HOME #..........................................................................

WORK #..........................................................................

FAX.................................................................................

EMAIL............................................................................

---

**NAME**............................................................................

ADDRESS.......................................................................

.....................................................................................

MOBILE # (Cell).............................................................

HOME #..........................................................................

WORK #..........................................................................

FAX.................................................................................

EMAIL............................................................................

---

**NAME**............................................................................

ADDRESS.......................................................................

.....................................................................................

MOBILE # (Cell).............................................................

HOME #..........................................................................

WORK #..........................................................................

FAX.................................................................................

EMAIL............................................................................

---

**NOTES:**

**NAME**................................................................................

ADDRESS.............................................................................

...........................................................................................

MOBILE # (Cell)..................................................................

HOME #.................................................................................

WORK #................................................................................

FAX........................................................................................

EMAIL...................................................................................

---

**NAME**................................................................................

ADDRESS.............................................................................

...........................................................................................

MOBILE # (Cell)..................................................................

HOME #.................................................................................

WORK #................................................................................

FAX........................................................................................

EMAIL...................................................................................

---

**NAME**................................................................................

ADDRESS.............................................................................

...........................................................................................

MOBILE # (Cell)..................................................................

HOME #.................................................................................

WORK #................................................................................

FAX........................................................................................

EMAIL...................................................................................

---

**NOTES:**

**NAME**............................................................................

ADDRESS.......................................................................

...................................................................................

MOBILE # (Cell)............................................................

HOME #.........................................................................

WORK #.........................................................................

FAX...............................................................................

EMAIL............................................................................

---

**NAME**............................................................................

ADDRESS.......................................................................

...................................................................................

MOBILE # (Cell)............................................................

HOME #.........................................................................

WORK #.........................................................................

FAX...............................................................................

EMAIL............................................................................

---

**NAME**............................................................................

ADDRESS.......................................................................

...................................................................................

MOBILE # (Cell)............................................................

HOME #.........................................................................

WORK #.........................................................................

FAX...............................................................................

EMAIL............................................................................

---

**NOTES:**

**NAME**.........................................................................................
ADDRESS........................................................................................
.......................................................................................................
MOBILE # (Cell)............................................................................
HOME #...........................................................................................
WORK #...........................................................................................
FAX.................................................................................................
EMAIL.............................................................................................

---

**NAME**.........................................................................................
ADDRESS........................................................................................
.......................................................................................................
MOBILE # (Cell)............................................................................
HOME #...........................................................................................
WORK #...........................................................................................
FAX.................................................................................................
EMAIL.............................................................................................

---

**NAME**.........................................................................................
ADDRESS........................................................................................
.......................................................................................................
MOBILE # (Cell)............................................................................
HOME #...........................................................................................
WORK #...........................................................................................
FAX.................................................................................................
EMAIL.............................................................................................

---

**NOTES:**

**NAME**..................................................................

ADDRESS...........................................................

..................................................................

MOBILE # (Cell)...................................................

HOME #............................................................

WORK #............................................................

FAX..................................................................

EMAIL..............................................................

---

**NAME**..................................................................

ADDRESS...........................................................

..................................................................

MOBILE # (Cell)...................................................

HOME #............................................................

WORK #............................................................

FAX..................................................................

EMAIL..............................................................

---

**NAME**..................................................................

ADDRESS...........................................................

..................................................................

MOBILE # (Cell)...................................................

HOME #............................................................

WORK #............................................................

FAX..................................................................

EMAIL..............................................................

---

**NOTES:**

**NAME**..............................................................................

ADDRESS.........................................................................

............................................................................................

MOBILE # (Cell)............................................................

HOME #..........................................................................

WORK #..........................................................................

FAX.................................................................................

EMAIL............................................................................

---

**NAME**..............................................................................

ADDRESS.........................................................................

............................................................................................

MOBILE # (Cell)............................................................

HOME #..........................................................................

WORK #..........................................................................

FAX.................................................................................

EMAIL............................................................................

---

**NAME**..............................................................................

ADDRESS.........................................................................

............................................................................................

MOBILE # (Cell)............................................................

HOME #..........................................................................

WORK #..........................................................................

FAX.................................................................................

EMAIL............................................................................

---

**NOTES:**

**NAME**............................................................................................

ADDRESS................................................................................................

................................................................................................

MOBILE # (Cell)................................................................................

HOME #................................................................................................

WORK #................................................................................................

FAX................................................................................................

EMAIL................................................................................................

---

**NAME**............................................................................................

ADDRESS................................................................................................

................................................................................................

MOBILE # (Cell)................................................................................

HOME #................................................................................................

WORK #................................................................................................

FAX................................................................................................

EMAIL................................................................................................

---

**NAME**............................................................................................

ADDRESS................................................................................................

................................................................................................

MOBILE # (Cell)................................................................................

HOME #................................................................................................

WORK #................................................................................................

FAX................................................................................................

EMAIL................................................................................................

---

**NOTES:**

**NAME**...............................................................................

ADDRESS............................................................................

.............................................................................................

MOBILE # (Cell).................................................................

HOME #...............................................................................

WORK #..............................................................................

FAX......................................................................................

EMAIL.................................................................................

---

**NAME**...............................................................................

ADDRESS............................................................................

.............................................................................................

MOBILE # (Cell).................................................................

HOME #...............................................................................

WORK #..............................................................................

FAX......................................................................................

EMAIL.................................................................................

---

**NAME**...............................................................................

ADDRESS............................................................................

.............................................................................................

MOBILE # (Cell).................................................................

HOME #...............................................................................

WORK #..............................................................................

FAX......................................................................................

EMAIL.................................................................................

---

**NOTES:**

**NAME**.................................................................................

ADDRESS.............................................................................

............................................................................................

MOBILE # (Cell)...................................................................

HOME #................................................................................

WORK #...............................................................................

FAX........................................................................................

EMAIL...................................................................................

---

**NAME**.................................................................................

ADDRESS.............................................................................

............................................................................................

MOBILE # (Cell)...................................................................

HOME #................................................................................

WORK #...............................................................................

FAX........................................................................................

EMAIL...................................................................................

---

**NAME**.................................................................................

ADDRESS.............................................................................

............................................................................................

MOBILE # (Cell)...................................................................

HOME #................................................................................

WORK #...............................................................................

FAX........................................................................................

EMAIL...................................................................................

---

**NOTES:**

**NAME**....................................................................................
ADDRESS.................................................................................
........................................................................................
MOBILE # (Cell)...................................................................
HOME #..................................................................................
WORK #.................................................................................
FAX..........................................................................................
EMAIL....................................................................................

---

**NAME**....................................................................................
ADDRESS.................................................................................
........................................................................................
MOBILE # (Cell)...................................................................
HOME #..................................................................................
WORK #.................................................................................
FAX..........................................................................................
EMAIL....................................................................................

---

**NAME**....................................................................................
ADDRESS.................................................................................
........................................................................................
MOBILE # (Cell)...................................................................
HOME #..................................................................................
WORK #.................................................................................
FAX..........................................................................................
EMAIL....................................................................................

---

**NOTES:**

**NAME**.................................................................................

ADDRESS..............................................................................

..............................................................................................

MOBILE # (Cell)..............................................................

HOME #............................................................................

WORK #............................................................................

FAX......................................................................................

EMAIL.................................................................................

---

**NAME**.................................................................................

ADDRESS..............................................................................

..............................................................................................

MOBILE # (Cell)..............................................................

HOME #............................................................................

WORK #............................................................................

FAX......................................................................................

EMAIL.................................................................................

---

**NAME**.................................................................................

ADDRESS..............................................................................

..............................................................................................

MOBILE # (Cell)..............................................................

HOME #............................................................................

WORK #............................................................................

FAX......................................................................................

EMAIL.................................................................................

---

**NOTES:**

NAME.....................................................................
ADDRESS..............................................................
.............................................................................
MOBILE # (Cell).................................................
HOME #................................................................
WORK #...............................................................
FAX.......................................................................
EMAIL..................................................................

NAME.....................................................................
ADDRESS..............................................................
.............................................................................
MOBILE # (Cell).................................................
HOME #................................................................
WORK #...............................................................
FAX.......................................................................
EMAIL..................................................................

NAME.....................................................................
ADDRESS..............................................................
.............................................................................
MOBILE # (Cell).................................................
HOME #................................................................
WORK #...............................................................
FAX.......................................................................
EMAIL..................................................................

NOTES:

**NAME**..................................................................................

ADDRESS............................................................................

..............................................................................................

MOBILE # (Cell)..............................................................

HOME #............................................................................

WORK #............................................................................

FAX....................................................................................

EMAIL..............................................................................

---

**NAME**..................................................................................

ADDRESS............................................................................

..............................................................................................

MOBILE # (Cell)..............................................................

HOME #............................................................................

WORK #............................................................................

FAX....................................................................................

EMAIL..............................................................................

---

**NAME**..................................................................................

ADDRESS............................................................................

..............................................................................................

MOBILE # (Cell)..............................................................

HOME #............................................................................

WORK #............................................................................

FAX....................................................................................

EMAIL..............................................................................

---

**NOTES:**

**NAME**..................................................................................

ADDRESS.............................................................................

.................................................................................................

MOBILE # (Cell)..............................................................

HOME #..........................................................................

WORK #..........................................................................

FAX.................................................................................

EMAIL.............................................................................

---

**NAME**..................................................................................

ADDRESS.............................................................................

.................................................................................................

MOBILE # (Cell)..............................................................

HOME #..........................................................................

WORK #..........................................................................

FAX.................................................................................

EMAIL.............................................................................

---

**NAME**..................................................................................

ADDRESS.............................................................................

.................................................................................................

MOBILE # (Cell)..............................................................

HOME #..........................................................................

WORK #..........................................................................

FAX.................................................................................

EMAIL.............................................................................

---

**NOTES:**

**NAME**............................................................................
ADDRESS.............................................................................
........................................................................................
MOBILE # (Cell)................................................................
HOME #.............................................................................
WORK #.............................................................................
FAX.....................................................................................
EMAIL................................................................................

**NAME**............................................................................
ADDRESS.............................................................................
........................................................................................
MOBILE # (Cell)................................................................
HOME #.............................................................................
WORK #.............................................................................
FAX.....................................................................................
EMAIL................................................................................

**NAME**............................................................................
ADDRESS.............................................................................
........................................................................................
MOBILE # (Cell)................................................................
HOME #.............................................................................
WORK #.............................................................................
FAX.....................................................................................
EMAIL................................................................................

**NOTES:**

**NAME**...........................................................................
ADDRESS........................................................................
.....................................................................................
MOBILE # (Cell)...........................................................
HOME #.........................................................................
WORK #.........................................................................
FAX...............................................................................
EMAIL............................................................................

---

**NAME**...........................................................................
ADDRESS........................................................................
.....................................................................................
MOBILE # (Cell)...........................................................
HOME #.........................................................................
WORK #.........................................................................
FAX...............................................................................
EMAIL............................................................................

---

**NAME**...........................................................................
ADDRESS........................................................................
.....................................................................................
MOBILE # (Cell)...........................................................
HOME #.........................................................................
WORK #.........................................................................
FAX...............................................................................
EMAIL............................................................................

---

**NOTES:**

**NAME**.................................................................................
ADDRESS............................................................................
.........................................................................................
MOBILE # (Cell).................................................................
HOME #.............................................................................
WORK #.............................................................................
FAX....................................................................................
EMAIL...............................................................................

---

**NAME**.................................................................................
ADDRESS............................................................................
.........................................................................................
MOBILE # (Cell).................................................................
HOME #.............................................................................
WORK #.............................................................................
FAX....................................................................................
EMAIL...............................................................................

---

**NAME**.................................................................................
ADDRESS............................................................................
.........................................................................................
MOBILE # (Cell).................................................................
HOME #.............................................................................
WORK #.............................................................................
FAX....................................................................................
EMAIL...............................................................................

---

**NOTES:**

**NAME**................................................................
ADDRESS...........................................................
........................................................................
MOBILE # (Cell)...............................................
HOME #.............................................................
WORK #.............................................................
FAX....................................................................
EMAIL................................................................

---

**NAME**................................................................
ADDRESS...........................................................
........................................................................
MOBILE # (Cell)...............................................
HOME #.............................................................
WORK #.............................................................
FAX....................................................................
EMAIL................................................................

---

**NAME**................................................................
ADDRESS...........................................................
........................................................................
MOBILE # (Cell)...............................................
HOME #.............................................................
WORK #.............................................................
FAX....................................................................
EMAIL................................................................

---

**NOTES:**

**NAME**...........................................................................

ADDRESS....................................................................

...............................................................................

MOBILE # (Cell)........................................................

HOME #.....................................................................

WORK #......................................................................

FAX.............................................................................

EMAIL........................................................................

---

**NAME**...........................................................................

ADDRESS....................................................................

...............................................................................

MOBILE # (Cell)........................................................

HOME #.....................................................................

WORK #......................................................................

FAX.............................................................................

EMAIL........................................................................

---

**NAME**...........................................................................

ADDRESS....................................................................

...............................................................................

MOBILE # (Cell)........................................................

HOME #.....................................................................

WORK #......................................................................

FAX.............................................................................

EMAIL........................................................................

---

**NOTES:**

**NAME**..............................................................................

ADDRESS...........................................................................

..........................................................................................

MOBILE # (Cell)................................................................

HOME #.............................................................................

WORK #.............................................................................

FAX....................................................................................

EMAIL................................................................................

---

**NAME**..............................................................................

ADDRESS...........................................................................

..........................................................................................

MOBILE # (Cell)................................................................

HOME #.............................................................................

WORK #.............................................................................

FAX....................................................................................

EMAIL................................................................................

---

**NAME**..............................................................................

ADDRESS...........................................................................

..........................................................................................

MOBILE # (Cell)................................................................

HOME #.............................................................................

WORK #.............................................................................

FAX....................................................................................

EMAIL................................................................................

---

**NOTES:**

**NAME**.............................................................................

ADDRESS......................................................................

........................................................................................

MOBILE # (Cell).......................................................

HOME #......................................................................

WORK #......................................................................

FAX..............................................................................

EMAIL.........................................................................

---

**NAME**.............................................................................

ADDRESS......................................................................

........................................................................................

MOBILE # (Cell).......................................................

HOME #......................................................................

WORK #......................................................................

FAX..............................................................................

EMAIL.........................................................................

---

**NAME**.............................................................................

ADDRESS......................................................................

........................................................................................

MOBILE # (Cell).......................................................

HOME #......................................................................

WORK #......................................................................

FAX..............................................................................

EMAIL.........................................................................

---

**NOTES:**

**NAME**...................................................................................

ADDRESS..............................................................................

.............................................................................................

MOBILE # (Cell)...............................................................

HOME #...............................................................................

WORK #...............................................................................

FAX.......................................................................................

EMAIL..................................................................................

---

**NAME**...................................................................................

ADDRESS..............................................................................

.............................................................................................

MOBILE # (Cell)...............................................................

HOME #...............................................................................

WORK #...............................................................................

FAX.......................................................................................

EMAIL..................................................................................

---

**NAME**...................................................................................

ADDRESS..............................................................................

.............................................................................................

MOBILE # (Cell)...............................................................

HOME #...............................................................................

WORK #...............................................................................

FAX.......................................................................................

EMAIL..................................................................................

---

**NOTES:**

**NAME**..............................................................................

ADDRESS.........................................................................

.......................................................................................

MOBILE # (Cell).............................................................

HOME #............................................................................

WORK #.............................................................................

FAX....................................................................................

EMAIL...............................................................................

---

**NAME**..............................................................................

ADDRESS.........................................................................

.......................................................................................

MOBILE # (Cell).............................................................

HOME #............................................................................

WORK #.............................................................................

FAX....................................................................................

EMAIL...............................................................................

---

**NAME**..............................................................................

ADDRESS.........................................................................

.......................................................................................

MOBILE # (Cell).............................................................

HOME #............................................................................

WORK #.............................................................................

FAX....................................................................................

EMAIL...............................................................................

---

**NOTES:**

**NAME**...................................................................................
ADDRESS..............................................................................
........................................................................................
MOBILE # (Cell)..................................................................
HOME #...............................................................................
WORK #...............................................................................
FAX.......................................................................................
EMAIL..................................................................................

---

**NAME**...................................................................................
ADDRESS..............................................................................
........................................................................................
MOBILE # (Cell)..................................................................
HOME #...............................................................................
WORK #...............................................................................
FAX.......................................................................................
EMAIL..................................................................................

---

**NAME**...................................................................................
ADDRESS..............................................................................
........................................................................................
MOBILE # (Cell)..................................................................
HOME #...............................................................................
WORK #...............................................................................
FAX.......................................................................................
EMAIL..................................................................................

---

**NOTES:**

**NAME**..................................................................................

ADDRESS...............................................................................

...............................................................................................

MOBILE # (Cell)....................................................................

HOME #..................................................................................

WORK #..................................................................................

FAX.........................................................................................

EMAIL....................................................................................

---

**NAME**..................................................................................

ADDRESS...............................................................................

...............................................................................................

MOBILE # (Cell)....................................................................

HOME #..................................................................................

WORK #..................................................................................

FAX.........................................................................................

EMAIL....................................................................................

---

**NAME**..................................................................................

ADDRESS...............................................................................

...............................................................................................

MOBILE # (Cell)....................................................................

HOME #..................................................................................

WORK #..................................................................................

FAX.........................................................................................

EMAIL....................................................................................

---

**NOTES:**

**NAME**..................................................................................

ADDRESS...............................................................................

...............................................................................................

MOBILE # (Cell)...................................................................

HOME #..................................................................................

WORK #...................................................................................

FAX...........................................................................................

EMAIL......................................................................................

---

**NAME**..................................................................................

ADDRESS...............................................................................

...............................................................................................

MOBILE # (Cell)...................................................................

HOME #..................................................................................

WORK #...................................................................................

FAX...........................................................................................

EMAIL......................................................................................

---

**NAME**..................................................................................

ADDRESS...............................................................................

...............................................................................................

MOBILE # (Cell)...................................................................

HOME #..................................................................................

WORK #...................................................................................

FAX...........................................................................................

EMAIL......................................................................................

---

**NOTES:**

**NAME**................................................................

ADDRESS.............................................................

...............................................................................

MOBILE # (Cell).................................................

HOME #.............................................................

WORK #.............................................................

FAX...................................................................

EMAIL...............................................................

---

**NAME**................................................................

ADDRESS.............................................................

...............................................................................

MOBILE # (Cell).................................................

HOME #.............................................................

WORK #.............................................................

FAX...................................................................

EMAIL...............................................................

---

**NAME**................................................................

ADDRESS.............................................................

...............................................................................

MOBILE # (Cell).................................................

HOME #.............................................................

WORK #.............................................................

FAX...................................................................

EMAIL...............................................................

---

**NOTES:**

**NAME**............................................................................

ADDRESS.........................................................................

..........................................................................................

MOBILE # (Cell)............................................................

HOME #..........................................................................

WORK #..........................................................................

FAX................................................................................

EMAIL............................................................................

---

**NAME**............................................................................

ADDRESS.........................................................................

..........................................................................................

MOBILE # (Cell)............................................................

HOME #..........................................................................

WORK #..........................................................................

FAX................................................................................

EMAIL............................................................................

---

**NAME**............................................................................

ADDRESS.........................................................................

..........................................................................................

MOBILE # (Cell)............................................................

HOME #..........................................................................

WORK #..........................................................................

FAX................................................................................

EMAIL............................................................................

---

**NOTES:**

**NAME**.................................................................................
ADDRESS.....................................................................................
.................................................................................................
MOBILE # (Cell).........................................................................
HOME #......................................................................................
WORK #......................................................................................
FAX.............................................................................................
EMAIL........................................................................................

---

**NAME**.................................................................................
ADDRESS.....................................................................................
.................................................................................................
MOBILE # (Cell).........................................................................
HOME #......................................................................................
WORK #......................................................................................
FAX.............................................................................................
EMAIL........................................................................................

---

**NAME**.................................................................................
ADDRESS.....................................................................................
.................................................................................................
MOBILE # (Cell).........................................................................
HOME #......................................................................................
WORK #......................................................................................
FAX.............................................................................................
EMAIL........................................................................................

---

<u>**NOTES:**</u>

**NAME**................................................................................

ADDRESS..........................................................................

.............................................................................................

MOBILE # (Cell)............................................................

HOME #...........................................................................

WORK #...........................................................................

FAX...................................................................................

EMAIL..............................................................................

---

**NAME**................................................................................

ADDRESS..........................................................................

.............................................................................................

MOBILE # (Cell)............................................................

HOME #...........................................................................

WORK #...........................................................................

FAX...................................................................................

EMAIL..............................................................................

---

**NAME**................................................................................

ADDRESS..........................................................................

.............................................................................................

MOBILE # (Cell)............................................................

HOME #...........................................................................

WORK #...........................................................................

FAX...................................................................................

EMAIL..............................................................................

---

**NOTES:**

**NAME**....................................................................................

ADDRESS..............................................................................

................................................................................................

MOBILE # (Cell)..................................................................

HOME #..................................................................................

WORK #..................................................................................

FAX.........................................................................................

EMAIL....................................................................................

---

**NAME**....................................................................................

ADDRESS..............................................................................

................................................................................................

MOBILE # (Cell)..................................................................

HOME #..................................................................................

WORK #..................................................................................

FAX.........................................................................................

EMAIL....................................................................................

---

**NAME**....................................................................................

ADDRESS..............................................................................

................................................................................................

MOBILE # (Cell)..................................................................

HOME #..................................................................................

WORK #..................................................................................

FAX.........................................................................................

EMAIL....................................................................................

---

**NOTES:**

**NAME**..............................................................................
ADDRESS.......................................................................
.......................................................................................
MOBILE # (Cell)...........................................................
HOME #.........................................................................
WORK #.........................................................................
FAX...............................................................................
EMAIL...........................................................................

---

**NAME**..............................................................................
ADDRESS.......................................................................
.......................................................................................
MOBILE # (Cell)...........................................................
HOME #.........................................................................
WORK #.........................................................................
FAX...............................................................................
EMAIL...........................................................................

---

**NAME**..............................................................................
ADDRESS.......................................................................
.......................................................................................
MOBILE # (Cell)...........................................................
HOME #.........................................................................
WORK #.........................................................................
FAX...............................................................................
EMAIL...........................................................................

---

**NOTES:**

**NAME**...........................................................................

ADDRESS..........................................................................

...............................................................................................

MOBILE # (Cell)..............................................................

HOME #...........................................................................

WORK #...........................................................................

FAX..................................................................................

EMAIL.............................................................................

---

**NAME**...........................................................................

ADDRESS..........................................................................

...............................................................................................

MOBILE # (Cell)..............................................................

HOME #...........................................................................

WORK #...........................................................................

FAX..................................................................................

EMAIL.............................................................................

---

**NAME**...........................................................................

ADDRESS..........................................................................

...............................................................................................

MOBILE # (Cell)..............................................................

HOME #...........................................................................

WORK #...........................................................................

FAX..................................................................................

EMAIL.............................................................................

---

**NOTES:**

**NAME**..................................................................................

ADDRESS...............................................................................

......................................................................................................

MOBILE # (Cell)....................................................................

HOME #..................................................................................

WORK #..................................................................................

FAX.........................................................................................

EMAIL...................................................................................

---

**NAME**..................................................................................

ADDRESS...............................................................................

......................................................................................................

MOBILE # (Cell)....................................................................

HOME #..................................................................................

WORK #..................................................................................

FAX.........................................................................................

EMAIL...................................................................................

---

**NAME**..................................................................................

ADDRESS...............................................................................

......................................................................................................

MOBILE # (Cell)....................................................................

HOME #..................................................................................

WORK #..................................................................................

FAX.........................................................................................

EMAIL...................................................................................

---

**NOTES:**

---

**NAME**..............................................................................
ADDRESS.........................................................................
...........................................................................................
MOBILE # (Cell).........................................................
HOME #........................................................................
WORK #.........................................................................
FAX...............................................................................
EMAIL...........................................................................

**NAME**..............................................................................
ADDRESS.........................................................................
...........................................................................................
MOBILE # (Cell).........................................................
HOME #........................................................................
WORK #.........................................................................
FAX...............................................................................
EMAIL...........................................................................

**NAME**..............................................................................
ADDRESS.........................................................................
...........................................................................................
MOBILE # (Cell).........................................................
HOME #........................................................................
WORK #.........................................................................
FAX...............................................................................
EMAIL...........................................................................

**NOTES:**

**NAME**.................................................................................................

ADDRESS.............................................................................................

.........................................................................................................

MOBILE # (Cell)...............................................................................

HOME #..............................................................................................

WORK #..............................................................................................

FAX......................................................................................................

EMAIL................................................................................................

---

**NAME**.................................................................................................

ADDRESS.............................................................................................

.........................................................................................................

MOBILE # (Cell)...............................................................................

HOME #..............................................................................................

WORK #..............................................................................................

FAX......................................................................................................

EMAIL................................................................................................

---

**NAME**.................................................................................................

ADDRESS.............................................................................................

.........................................................................................................

MOBILE # (Cell)...............................................................................

HOME #..............................................................................................

WORK #..............................................................................................

FAX......................................................................................................

EMAIL................................................................................................

---

**NOTES:**

**NAME**.................................................................................

ADDRESS........................................................................

.......................................................................................

MOBILE # (Cell)...........................................................

HOME #..........................................................................

WORK #..........................................................................

FAX...................................................................................

EMAIL.............................................................................

**NAME**.................................................................................

ADDRESS........................................................................

.......................................................................................

MOBILE # (Cell)...........................................................

HOME #..........................................................................

WORK #..........................................................................

FAX...................................................................................

EMAIL.............................................................................

**NAME**.................................................................................

ADDRESS........................................................................

.......................................................................................

MOBILE # (Cell)...........................................................

HOME #..........................................................................

WORK #..........................................................................

FAX...................................................................................

EMAIL.............................................................................

**NOTES:**

**NAME**..............................................................................

ADDRESS.........................................................................

....................................................................................

MOBILE # (Cell)...........................................................

HOME #..........................................................................

WORK #...........................................................................

FAX.................................................................................

EMAIL.............................................................................

---

**NAME**..............................................................................

ADDRESS.........................................................................

....................................................................................

MOBILE # (Cell)...........................................................

HOME #..........................................................................

WORK #...........................................................................

FAX.................................................................................

EMAIL.............................................................................

---

**NAME**..............................................................................

ADDRESS.........................................................................

....................................................................................

MOBILE # (Cell)...........................................................

HOME #..........................................................................

WORK #...........................................................................

FAX.................................................................................

EMAIL.............................................................................

---

**NOTES:**

**NAME**..........................................................................

ADDRESS..........................................................................

.........................................................................................

MOBILE # (Cell).............................................................

HOME #............................................................................

WORK #............................................................................

FAX....................................................................................

EMAIL..............................................................................

---

**NAME**..........................................................................

ADDRESS..........................................................................

.........................................................................................

MOBILE # (Cell).............................................................

HOME #............................................................................

WORK #............................................................................

FAX....................................................................................

EMAIL..............................................................................

---

**NAME**..........................................................................

ADDRESS..........................................................................

.........................................................................................

MOBILE # (Cell).............................................................

HOME #............................................................................

WORK #............................................................................

FAX....................................................................................

EMAIL..............................................................................

---

**NOTES:**

**NAME**.................................................................................

ADDRESS.........................................................................

...............................................................................................

MOBILE # (Cell)...........................................................

HOME #.........................................................................

WORK #.........................................................................

FAX.................................................................................

EMAIL............................................................................

---

**NAME**.................................................................................

ADDRESS.........................................................................

...............................................................................................

MOBILE # (Cell)...........................................................

HOME #.........................................................................

WORK #.........................................................................

FAX.................................................................................

EMAIL............................................................................

---

**NAME**.................................................................................

ADDRESS.........................................................................

...............................................................................................

MOBILE # (Cell)...........................................................

HOME #.........................................................................

WORK #.........................................................................

FAX.................................................................................

EMAIL............................................................................

---

<u>NOTES:</u>

---

**NAME**......................................................................

ADDRESS.................................................................

..............................................................................

MOBILE # (Cell)....................................................

HOME #..................................................................

WORK #...................................................................

FAX.........................................................................

EMAIL....................................................................

---

**NAME**......................................................................

ADDRESS.................................................................

..............................................................................

MOBILE # (Cell)....................................................

HOME #..................................................................

WORK #...................................................................

FAX.........................................................................

EMAIL....................................................................

---

**NAME**......................................................................

ADDRESS.................................................................

..............................................................................

MOBILE # (Cell)....................................................

HOME #..................................................................

WORK #...................................................................

FAX.........................................................................

EMAIL....................................................................

---

**NOTES:**

**NAME**.................................................................................

ADDRESS..........................................................................

..........................................................................................

MOBILE # (Cell).............................................................

HOME #..............................................................................

WORK #...............................................................................

FAX......................................................................................

EMAIL................................................................................

---

**NAME**.................................................................................

ADDRESS..........................................................................

..........................................................................................

MOBILE # (Cell).............................................................

HOME #..............................................................................

WORK #...............................................................................

FAX......................................................................................

EMAIL................................................................................

---

**NAME**.................................................................................

ADDRESS..........................................................................

..........................................................................................

MOBILE # (Cell).............................................................

HOME #..............................................................................

WORK #...............................................................................

FAX......................................................................................

EMAIL................................................................................

---

**NOTES:**

**NAME**............................................................................

ADDRESS..................................................................................

.......................................................................................

MOBILE # (Cell)........................................................................

HOME #.................................................................................

WORK #................................................................................

FAX.....................................................................................

EMAIL..................................................................................

---

**NAME**............................................................................

ADDRESS..................................................................................

.......................................................................................

MOBILE # (Cell)........................................................................

HOME #.................................................................................

WORK #................................................................................

FAX.....................................................................................

EMAIL..................................................................................

---

**NAME**............................................................................

ADDRESS..................................................................................

.......................................................................................

MOBILE # (Cell)........................................................................

HOME #.................................................................................

WORK #................................................................................

FAX.....................................................................................

EMAIL..................................................................................

---

<u>**NOTES:**</u>

**NAME**..................................................................................

ADDRESS..............................................................................

..................................................................................

MOBILE # (Cell)...................................................................

HOME #................................................................................

WORK #................................................................................

FAX........................................................................................

EMAIL....................................................................................

---

**NAME**..................................................................................

ADDRESS..............................................................................

..................................................................................

MOBILE # (Cell)...................................................................

HOME #................................................................................

WORK #................................................................................

FAX........................................................................................

EMAIL....................................................................................

---

**NAME**..................................................................................

ADDRESS..............................................................................

..................................................................................

MOBILE # (Cell)...................................................................

HOME #................................................................................

WORK #................................................................................

FAX........................................................................................

EMAIL....................................................................................

---

**NOTES:**

**NAME**..................................................................................

ADDRESS...........................................................................

...............................................................................................

MOBILE # (Cell).............................................................

HOME #.............................................................................

WORK #.............................................................................

FAX.....................................................................................

EMAIL................................................................................

**NAME**..................................................................................

ADDRESS...........................................................................

...............................................................................................

MOBILE # (Cell).............................................................

HOME #.............................................................................

WORK #.............................................................................

FAX.....................................................................................

EMAIL................................................................................

**NAME**..................................................................................

ADDRESS...........................................................................

...............................................................................................

MOBILE # (Cell).............................................................

HOME #.............................................................................

WORK #.............................................................................

FAX.....................................................................................

EMAIL................................................................................

**NOTES:**

**NAME**..................................................................................
ADDRESS.............................................................................
..................................................................................................
MOBILE # (Cell).................................................................
HOME #...............................................................................
WORK #..............................................................................
FAX......................................................................................
EMAIL.................................................................................

---

**NAME**..................................................................................
ADDRESS.............................................................................
..................................................................................................
MOBILE # (Cell).................................................................
HOME #...............................................................................
WORK #..............................................................................
FAX......................................................................................
EMAIL.................................................................................

---

**NAME**..................................................................................
ADDRESS.............................................................................
..................................................................................................
MOBILE # (Cell).................................................................
HOME #...............................................................................
WORK #..............................................................................
FAX......................................................................................
EMAIL.................................................................................

---

**NOTES:**

**NAME**.................................................................................

ADDRESS...........................................................................

.............................................................................................

MOBILE # (Cell)...............................................................

HOME #.............................................................................

WORK #.............................................................................

FAX...................................................................................

EMAIL...............................................................................

---

**NAME**.................................................................................

ADDRESS...........................................................................

.............................................................................................

MOBILE # (Cell)...............................................................

HOME #.............................................................................

WORK #.............................................................................

FAX...................................................................................

EMAIL...............................................................................

---

**NAME**.................................................................................

ADDRESS...........................................................................

.............................................................................................

MOBILE # (Cell)...............................................................

HOME #.............................................................................

WORK #.............................................................................

FAX...................................................................................

EMAIL...............................................................................

---

**NOTES:**

**NAME**...............................................................................

ADDRESS..............................................................................

.........................................................................................

MOBILE # (Cell)..................................................................

HOME #................................................................................

WORK #................................................................................

FAX.......................................................................................

EMAIL..................................................................................

---

**NAME**...............................................................................

ADDRESS..............................................................................

.........................................................................................

MOBILE # (Cell)..................................................................

HOME #................................................................................

WORK #................................................................................

FAX.......................................................................................

EMAIL..................................................................................

---

**NAME**...............................................................................

ADDRESS..............................................................................

.........................................................................................

MOBILE # (Cell)..................................................................

HOME #................................................................................

WORK #................................................................................

FAX.......................................................................................

EMAIL..................................................................................

---

**NOTES:**

**NAME**..................................................................

ADDRESS.........................................................

..............................................................................

MOBILE # (Cell)...........................................................

HOME #.................................................................

WORK #................................................................

FAX........................................................................

EMAIL...................................................................

---

**NAME**..................................................................

ADDRESS.........................................................

..............................................................................

MOBILE # (Cell)...........................................................

HOME #.................................................................

WORK #................................................................

FAX........................................................................

EMAIL...................................................................

---

**NAME**..................................................................

ADDRESS.........................................................

..............................................................................

MOBILE # (Cell)...........................................................

HOME #.................................................................

WORK #................................................................

FAX........................................................................

EMAIL...................................................................

---

**NOTES:**

**NAME**..................................................................................
ADDRESS.............................................................................
....................................................................................................
MOBILE # (Cell)...............................................................
HOME #.............................................................................
WORK #.............................................................................
FAX....................................................................................
EMAIL................................................................................

---

**NAME**..................................................................................
ADDRESS.............................................................................
....................................................................................................
MOBILE # (Cell)...............................................................
HOME #.............................................................................
WORK #.............................................................................
FAX....................................................................................
EMAIL................................................................................

---

**NAME**..................................................................................
ADDRESS.............................................................................
....................................................................................................
MOBILE # (Cell)...............................................................
HOME #.............................................................................
WORK #.............................................................................
FAX....................................................................................
EMAIL................................................................................

---

**NOTES:**

**NAME**...................................................................................

ADDRESS..............................................................................

.............................................................................................

MOBILE # (Cell).................................................................

HOME #..................................................................................

WORK #.................................................................................

FAX...........................................................................................

EMAIL.....................................................................................

---

**NAME**...................................................................................

ADDRESS..............................................................................

.............................................................................................

MOBILE # (Cell).................................................................

HOME #..................................................................................

WORK #.................................................................................

FAX...........................................................................................

EMAIL.....................................................................................

---

**NAME**...................................................................................

ADDRESS..............................................................................

.............................................................................................

MOBILE # (Cell).................................................................

HOME #..................................................................................

WORK #.................................................................................

FAX...........................................................................................

EMAIL.....................................................................................

---

**NOTES:**

**NAME**..........................................................................................

ADDRESS.....................................................................................

.............................................................................................

MOBILE # (Cell).........................................................................

HOME #.....................................................................................

WORK #.....................................................................................

FAX............................................................................................

EMAIL.......................................................................................

---

**NAME**..........................................................................................

ADDRESS.....................................................................................

.............................................................................................

MOBILE # (Cell).........................................................................

HOME #.....................................................................................

WORK #.....................................................................................

FAX............................................................................................

EMAIL.......................................................................................

---

**NAME**..........................................................................................

ADDRESS.....................................................................................

.............................................................................................

MOBILE # (Cell).........................................................................

HOME #.....................................................................................

WORK #.....................................................................................

FAX............................................................................................

EMAIL.......................................................................................

---

<u>**NOTES:**</u>

**NAME**..................................................................................

ADDRESS...........................................................................

....................................................................................................

MOBILE # (Cell)...........................................................................

HOME #..................................................................................

WORK #.................................................................................

FAX......................................................................................

EMAIL...................................................................................

---

**NAME**..................................................................................

ADDRESS...........................................................................

....................................................................................................

MOBILE # (Cell)...........................................................................

HOME #..................................................................................

WORK #.................................................................................

FAX......................................................................................

EMAIL...................................................................................

---

**NAME**..................................................................................

ADDRESS...........................................................................

....................................................................................................

MOBILE # (Cell)...........................................................................

HOME #..................................................................................

WORK #.................................................................................

FAX......................................................................................

EMAIL...................................................................................

---

**NOTES:**

**NAME**.......................................................................................
ADDRESS....................................................................................
..................................................................................................
MOBILE # (Cell)........................................................................
HOME #.....................................................................................
WORK #.....................................................................................
FAX............................................................................................
EMAIL.......................................................................................

---

**NAME**.......................................................................................
ADDRESS....................................................................................
..................................................................................................
MOBILE # (Cell)........................................................................
HOME #.....................................................................................
WORK #.....................................................................................
FAX............................................................................................
EMAIL.......................................................................................

---

**NAME**.......................................................................................
ADDRESS....................................................................................
..................................................................................................
MOBILE # (Cell)........................................................................
HOME #.....................................................................................
WORK #.....................................................................................
FAX............................................................................................
EMAIL.......................................................................................

---

**NOTES:**

**NAME**....................................................................
ADDRESS.............................................................
............................................................................
MOBILE # (Cell)................................................
HOME #.................................................................
WORK #.................................................................
FAX........................................................................
EMAIL...................................................................

---

**NAME**....................................................................
ADDRESS.............................................................
............................................................................
MOBILE # (Cell)................................................
HOME #.................................................................
WORK #.................................................................
FAX........................................................................
EMAIL...................................................................

---

**NAME**....................................................................
ADDRESS.............................................................
............................................................................
MOBILE # (Cell)................................................
HOME #.................................................................
WORK #.................................................................
FAX........................................................................
EMAIL...................................................................

---

**NOTES:**